# RECEIVING THE WORD OF THE LORD

## BRINGING LIFE TO YOUR PROPHETIC WORD

# RECEIVING THE WORD OF THE LORD

## BRINGING LIFE TO YOUR PROPHETIC WORD

CHUCK D. PIERCE
AND
REBECCA WAGNER SYTSEMA

WAGNER
INSTITUTE
PUBLICATIONS

*Receiving the Word of the Lord*
Copyright © 1999
by Chuck D. Pierce and Rebecca Wagner Sytsema
ISBN 0-9667481-2-3

Second printing: July, 1999


Published by
Wagner Institute for Practical Ministry
P.O. Box 62958
Colorado Springs, CO  80962-2958

# TABLE OF CONTENTS

# INTRODUCTION

Hearing the voice of God is not as difficult as some might think. I have found that many of God's people are hearing Him, but have not perceived that it is His voice. To perceive means to take hold of, feel, comprehend, grasp mentally, recognize, observe, or become aware of something by discerning. We must learn to perceive God's voice, which will help us understand His will for our lives. Acting upon what we have discerned as His voice until it becomes a reality is the key to a successful Christian life.

To commune with a holy God—you talk to Him and He to you—is the highest privilege we have on earth. My own life has become one of hearing the Lord's voice, not just for myself but for others as well. My greatest desire is for each person to hear God's voice, embrace His word, and fulfill the destiny God has for them.

I pray that this simple book will give you the principles of hearing God through prophecy, show you how to test and evaluate the prophetic word, and help you know what to do with what God has spoken to you. As you read this book may you recognize the Voice that gives you life and life abundantly!

Chuck D. Pierce
Colorado Springs, Colorado

# CHAPTER ONE

# KNOWING GOD SPEAKS

When I first became aware that God had a voice and actually spoke to people, I was eight years old. My godly grandmother would take me to a little Baptist church in East Texas where we lived. In that church was a lady named Mrs. Grimes who would do a very peculiar thing. Right in the middle of the preacher's message, Mrs. Grimes would stand up and wave her hands. Being a Baptist church, this was very unusual behavior. Yet the preacher would stop his message and ask her what was happening. Mrs. Grimes would say, "The Lord is speaking to me!" Then the pastor would say, "Tell us what He's saying." Then Mrs. Grimes would begin to tell us what she was hearing from the Spirit of God and how it affected the church.

It totally fascinated me that this God of whom the preacher talked could really speak to people today. I would look up at my grandmother and say, "If God can speak to that woman, I want Him to speak to me." My grandmother would look down at a typically wild eight-year-old boy and say, "You will have to learn to be quiet and sit still for God to ever say anything to you!"

## MY DAY OF SALVATION

From that point on there was no question in my mind that God had a voice. I had seen it through Mrs. Grimes, and I saw it in the biblical stories I heard in Sunday School. Still, I had never heard Him speak directly to me. When I was eleven, the Spirit of the Lord came to me in a church service and clearly said, "This is your day." It was as if I followed His Spirit up to the altar and surrendered my life, as well as I knew how at that point, based upon His voice speaking to me.

As I studied the Bible later on, I saw that God has a day of salvation for each one of us (see 2 Cor. 6:2). I saw that we all could come into our day of salvation by hearing God's voice speak into our spirit that was dead in trespasses. As we respond to His voice and allow His voice to illuminate truth in our darkened spirit, we come into our day of salvation. In fact, none of us has been saved without the voice of God prompting us. We may not have heard an audible voice, but because only God can illuminate the truth of salvation, everyone who has had a salvation experience and knows Jesus as their Lord and Savior has heard God's voice, whether or not they understood it at the time!

## "I WILL RESTORE"

Even though I had been saved, I had a difficult, often traumatic, and abusive childhood. Our family had suffered great loss and anguish. But when I was 18, the Lord clearly spoke to me and said, "I will restore all that you have lost." I had never seen that in the Bible, but as I read more deeply, I learned that God's voice had the power to restore (see Joel 2:25). My whole life changed from that instant. God has healed, delivered, and restored me in miraculous ways.[1] God's voice has great power to bring us out of the ruins of our past and set us on the course He has ordained for our lives.

## GOD'S VOICE IS CREATIVE

In the account of creation that we read in Genesis, we see that the creative instrument God used again and again was His voice. God *spoke* into chaos and light came into being. He *spoke* again and light divided from darkness, creating day and night. The power of His voice created the heavens and earth, and the abundance of creatures that filled the earth and seas.

God's voice is so powerful that it can divide substance. From the power of His voice, substance could be made into a different form. God made the ground from His creative voice and from that ground He formed human beings. Our very being is, therefore, a product of His creative voice.

## JESUS SPEAKS

Jesus was God as man come to earth to redeem the human race and to present the full character of God to us. Part of that character was the power of His voice. When Jesus spoke, things would happen. His public ministry began in John 2 when He and His mother attended a wedding. As the wedding feast ran short of wine, Jesus' mother told the servants, "Whatever He says to you, do it" (Jn. 2:5). It was Jesus' creative voice (the creative voice of God through Jesus as God and man) that changed the water to wine.

Let's look at how Jesus spoke to raise Lazarus from the dead. He spoke to the grave and to the shroud of death surrounding Lazarus and commanded them to loose Lazarus and let him go. When Jesus spoke, life processes once again began to flow through Lazarus after four days of death and decay.

## THE HOLY SPIRIT SPEAKS TO AND THROUGH

The Holy Spirit was released to operate in a new way in the transitional chapter of John 20. Jesus had already been crucified, died, and raised from the dead, but had not yet ascended to heaven. Jesus knew that He had to equip His disciples with power to accomplish their role on earth because He was now leaving to be with the Father. So in John 20:22 we read that "He breathed on them, and said to them, 'Receive the Holy Spirit.'"

As the Holy Spirit was released to them, He began to speak *to* them and *through* them on an ongoing basis. The Holy Spirit spoke many times to them, including when Peter was instructed to go to the house of Cornelius.  But prophecy was birthed in a whole new way as the Holy Spirit began to speak *through* them on a consistent basis.  In Acts, the account of Stephen records, "and they were not able to resist the wisdom and the Spirit by which he spoke" (Acts 6:10).  Here the Holy Spirit spoke *through* Stephen.

When God formed us with His creative voice, He made us in His image, according to His likeness, and gave us dominion over all the earth (see Gen. 1:26).  Because we are created in His image, and have been redeemed by Christ, therefore we have the ability, through the power of the Holy Spirit, to be the voice of God on the earth.  That is what prophecy is all about.

---

[1] A more complete account of this story is written in my book, *Possessing Your Inheritance*, (Renew Books, 1999.)

CHAPTER TWO

# WHAT IS PROPHECY?

*And it shall come to pass in the last days, says God,*
*that I will pour out of My Spirit on all flesh; your sons and*
*your daughters shall prophesy, your young men shall see*
*visions, your old men shall dream dreams (Acts 2:17).*

## IS PROPHECY FOR TODAY?

Most Christians in the United States today grew up in churches that did not embrace the idea of God speaking to us today. We were taught "cessationism," which means that the power gifts of healing, tongues, interpretation of tongues, miracles, and the like all ceased to function sometime in the first century. One of the gifts that supposedly stopped functioning was prophecy. What that basically means is that God said all He had to say by 95 A.D., and He has been silent ever since.

Those that hold to this line of thinking believe that prophecy passed away when the Scriptures were completed. They base their belief on 1 Corinthians 13:8-9 which says that prophecy, tongues, and knowledge will pass away. However, Paul encourages us in the following chapter to desire prophecy (1 Cor. 14:1).

He did not say that these gifts would be replaced by any others, nor that they would pass away before the second coming of Christ.

In fact, in Ephesians 4 Paul writes, "And He Himself gave some to be apostles, some prophets, some evangelists, and some pastors and teachers, for the equipping of the saints for the work of ministry, for the edifying of the body of Christ, *till we all come to the unity of the faith and of the knowledge of the Son of God, to a perfect man, to the measure of the stature of the fullness of Christ*" (Eph. 4:11-13, italics added). In this passage we see that these gifts have been given *until* we come to unity and we reach the stature of the fullness of Christ. At no time in the history of the Church have we achieved those things. Therefore, based on Paul's own words, those gifts, including prophecy, are still in operation today.

## HOW CAN I KNOW THE WILL OF GOD?

The Bible makes it very clear that God has a purpose and a plan for our lives. Any biblical scholar will agree that that did not end in the first century. But if we have a God that won't speak to us, it can be hard to discern what that plan is. Many of us have read books or heard messages on knowing the will of God. Those books are all filled with good principles that we can follow. Yet, the fact is that the Bible only gives one real principle to follow in trying to determine what God's will is for us. In the Bible, when someone wanted to know the will of God, they asked Him—and He told them!

God *does* speak to His people. But if we are so entrenched in a mindset that says that God does not speak today, we can often write it off as imagination. The truth is that the prophetic is not an optional extra in the Christian life. The prophetic is not an optional extra in the Church. Amos 3:7 even goes so far as to say, "Surely the Lord GOD does nothing, unless He reveals His secret to His servants the prophets."

Throughout the Bible, God communicated with His people. In 1 Corinthians 12, Paul reminds the Gentiles that they once worshiped mute idols. What a foolish thing to worship something that cannot communicate! Our God, however, is not like the mute idols. Our God is constantly pouring out new revelation, continually speaking to His people. He is a God who loves us enough that He wants to enter into communication with us.

## WHAT IS PROPHECY?

The definition of prophecy is simple. Prophecy is speaking forth the mind of God under the inspiration of the Holy Spirit. Prophecy is the outflow of the heart and the very nature of God. Revelation 19:10 says that the testimony of Jesus is the spirit of prophecy. Jesus cares about His Church and He, therefore, has things He wants to communicate to His Church. Those communications come by way of the Holy Spirit. That is prophecy. It is what Jesus is saying to His Church.

The testimony of Jesus, which is prophecy, is not only a corporate promise. Jesus says that His sheep know His voice (Jn. 10:4). If you are one of His sheep, you have the capability, the capacity, and the privilege of hearing the voice of your Shepherd that comes through the Holy Spirit.

## UNDERSTANDING THE PROPHETS

Throughout the Bible we find several Hebrew and Greek words that are translated as "prophet." In understanding how prophecy works today, it is helpful to know the different types of prophets and prophecy taught in God's Word. Let's take a look at some of the various names the Bible uses to describe the prophet:

**1. Nabi.** This is the general Hebrew word for prophet. It means one who proclaims, announces, declares, utters communications, a spokesman, or a heralder. This word also means a supernatural message that bubbles up or springs forth. *Nabi* is the word used in 1 Samuel 3:20, "And all Israel from Dan to Beersheba knew that Samuel had been established as a prophet of the LORD." It can be either masculine or feminine and can refer to either a prophet of God, or a false prophet who brings messages that are contrary to God's character or will.

**2. Roeh.** This Hebrew word means "seer." An example is 1 Samuel 9:9, "Come, let us go to the seer." A seer is probably the most misunderstood of the prophetic types. They are the ones who have visions or visual impressions. These types of prophets can look at something and receive a supernatural message through that image. God asked many of the prophets in Scripture, "What do you see?" The Lord has often used this method of communicating with me.

**3. Hazon.** This Hebrew word is translated as watchman. Here are some biblical examples of watchmen: "Also, I set watchmen over you, saying, 'Listen to the sound of the trumpet!'" (Jer. 6:17); "Son of man, I have made you a watchman for the house of Israel; therefore hear a word from My mouth, and give them warning from Me." A watchman sees what is coming. A watchman also watches after the word of the Lord and intercedes until it is accomplished. In 1 Kings 18, Elijah released the word of the Lord to Ahab, which was that it would not rain for 3½ years. At the end of that time Elijah went into intercession until he "saw" the cloud that represented God's change of seasons. Elijah was acting as a watchman.

**4. Prophetes.** This Greek word signifies one who speaks for another, especially one who speaks for God. These are ones who "forthtell," which means that they speak forth a living message from God for the hour. In this context, the prophet is using interpretive gifts to forthtell the will and counsel of God. This word also signifies one who can "foretell," or give insights into future events. In this context, the prophet is using predictive gifts. This is the kind of prophet mentioned in Matthew 2:5, who wrote that the Savior would come out of the city of Bethlehem.

**5. Nataph.** This Hebrew word means to preach, to drop from heaven, or to speak by (heavenly) inspiration. This type of prophesying is that which is generally done from a pulpit or in a public place, or a prophetic word that is given in the form of an exhortation. The word *nataph* is used in Micah 2:6, Micah 2:11, and Zechariah 13:3.

## THE KEY TO PROPHECY

The Holy Spirit is our key to hearing God. Throughout the Bible, in both the Old and New Testaments, whenever the Holy Spirit came, prophecy flowed. Here are just a few examples: "Then the Spirit of the LORD will come upon you, and you will prophesy" (1 Sam. 10:6); "The Spirit of God came upon the messengers of Saul, and they also prophesied" (1 Sam. 19:20); "And it happened, when the Spirit rested upon them, that they prophesied" (Num. 11:25); "And when Paul had laid hands on them, the Holy Spirit came upon them, and they spoke with tongues and prophesied" (Acts 19:6).

But the Holy Spirit's ministry through prophecy did not end in the first century! In many accounts of revival throughout the Church's history, when the Holy Spirit came in power, prophecy broke lose. In fact, one of the signs of the Spirit's presence is prophecy.

## WHY IS PROPHECY IMPORTANT?

Prophecy is important because God tells us it is. It is just that simple. Here are three reasons we find in the Bible that help us understand God's heart toward this important gift:

**1. We are to seek to prophesy.** "Pursue love, and desire spiritual gifts, but especially that you may prophesy" (1 Cor. 14:1). In the King James version, this verse says that we are to covet prophecy. Do you know that prophecy is the only thing in all the Bible we are supposed to covet? And what happens when you covet something? You think about it all the time. You desire it. You think about what you could do to get it. That's how we are supposed to seek prophecy.

Revelation 2 and 3 have the words of Jesus to many different churches. Jesus gives different admonishments, different promises, and different messages to each of the seven churches listed in those passages. The one thing that does not differ from church to church, however, is Jesus' command: "He who has an ear, let him hear what the Spirit is saying." We are to hear what the Spirit is saying. We are to seek prophecy.

**2. God warns us not to reject prophecy.** "Do not despise prophecies. Test all things; hold fast what is good" (1 Thes. 5:20-21). When Paul wrote to the Thessalonian church, they were still young in the Lord. They were just starting out. When something is in the beginning stages, things may not always happen the way they should. Out of immaturity and lack of understanding, flaky things can happen. When flakiness springs up, there is a tendency to say that something (in this case prophecy) is more trouble than it's worth. But Paul says no. Don't shut it down. Don't quench the Spirit. Let it happen, test everything, and hold on to what is good.

The Bible also tells us not to despise tongues. The relationship between prophecy and tongues is often misunderstood. Simply put, when a tongue is interpreted, it becomes prophecy.

**3. Prophecy releases the life and power of God.** As we saw in Chapter One, the word of God has creative power. When Ezekiel saw the dry, dead bones, the Lord told him to prophesy to them.

"So I prophesied as I was commanded; and as I prophesied, there was a noise, and suddenly a rattling; and the bones came together, bone to bone. Indeed, as I looked, the sinews and the flesh came upon them, and the skin covered them over; but there was no breath in them. Then He said to me, 'Prophesy to the breath, prophesy, son of man, and say to the breath, 'Thus says the Lord GOD: Come from the four winds, O breath, and breathe on these slain, that they may live.' ' So I prophesied as He commanded me, and breath came into them, and they lived, and stood upon their feet, an exceedingly great army" (Ezek. 37:7-10).

When the prophetic word of God goes forth, it doesn't just enlighten you, it doesn't just give you information, it releases life and power. Prophecy changes situations!

## UNDERSTANDING THE GIFT

The Holy Spirit equips us to accomplish God's purposes on earth. This is what 1 Corinthians 12, 13, and 14 are about. Too often these chapters are separated from one another in the teaching we receive. But the fact is that they were written together and they flow together to help give us an understanding of spiritual gifts and how they are to operate in the body of Christ. Let's look at this passage in light of the gift of prophecy.

The body of Christ works in just that way—it is a body, each part having a function and purpose that assists the whole in operating correctly. This is explained in some detail in 1 Corinthians 12. There are, however, certain gifts that are to be desired in the body, one of which is prophecy.

From that point, Paul immediately goes into a discourse on the outworkings and importance of love. He goes so far as to say, "And though I have the gift of prophecy...but have not love, I am nothing" (1 Cor. 13:2).

From there he moves on to say, "pursue love, and desire spiritual gifts, but especially that you may prophesy" (1 Cor. 14:1). Godly prophecy cannot be separated from love. In fact, true prophecy flows from a heart of love, even if the word is one of correction. The basis for understanding the gift of prophecy is understanding issues of love.

CHAPTER THREE

# THE FUNCTIONS, PROCESS, AND VALUE OF PROPHECY

## FIVE DYNAMIC FUNCTIONS OF PROPHECY

Having laid out a basic understanding of what prophecy is, let's now take a look at what prophecy does. From 1 Corinthians 14, we see that there are different purposes for prophecy. Here is a list of five functions that prophecy is meant to accomplish:

**1. Comfort.** To comfort is to soothe, reassure, bring cheer, bring a feeling of relief from pain or anxiety, lessen one's grief or distress, and give strength and hope by means of kindness and thoughtful attention. God is the "Father of mercies and God of all comfort, who comforts us in all our tribulation, that we may be able to comfort those who are in any trouble, with the comfort with which we ourselves are comforted by God. For as the sufferings of Christ abound in us, so our consolation also abounds through Christ" (2 Cor. 1:3-5).

God longs to comfort His hurting children. He longs to speak to them in a way that produces strength and hope. This is one of the very basic functions of prophecy that all believers should both receive and deliver to others. A prophetic word of comfort spoken at the right moment can break the back of discouragement, hopelessness, and anguish!

**2. Edification.** To edify means to instruct, benefit, uplift, enlighten, or build up. 1 Corinthians 14 is filled with the correlation between prophecy and edification, which is the building up of Christian character. A prophetic word, therefore, may contain elements of teaching or it may bring new revelation to our minds and spirits. The word may bring specific instruction. The word may bring a sense of strengthening a place in our lives that has been in desolation or ruins. All of these are types of edification we might receive from a prophetic word.

1 Corinthians 8:1 tells us that love edifies. Because love is the basis for prophecy, all true prophecies, therefore, have an element of edification.

**3. Exhortation.** To exhort is to urge, advise, caution, admonish, recommend, or warn. A prophetic word that exhorts, therefore, can either build up or tear down. Exhortation may be difficult to receive. It may not be the word of comfort for which we were hoping. Even so, words of exhortation are vital in that they bring forth the ultimate purpose of God. Even a difficult word of exhortation that is delivered in the right spirit leaves us feeling a sense of relief and freedom. Prophecy should not leave us with confusion or condemnation, but rather with direction and a way of escape from bondage.

**4. Redemptive.** One of the basic and most beautiful functions of prophecy is seeing redemption come into lives. God's heart revealed throughout the Bible is to redeem us from the power of sin and death. Since prophecy is speaking forth the mind of God, under the inspiration of the Holy Spirit, the logical conclusion is that prophecy should be redemptive.

About a decade ago, a young man named Jon received just such a word from my good friend, Cindy Jacobs. Jon was a good husband and father who was responsible and provided well for his family. He attended church every Sunday and tried his best to follow God. Yet Jon was a closet alcoholic. He was a functional alcoholic, which means that even when he was drunk, few around him knew it. Because he could handle liquor well, he was able to keep secret the fact that he could barely make it through a day without drinking. In addition, he was addicted to chewing tobacco. He knew these things were wrong and had sought God for healing.

During this time in his life, he attended a weekend retreat which was being taught by Cindy. One night Jon sat quietly in the back while Cindy began giving personal words of prophecy. He felt that God would have nothing to say to him. To his amazement, Cindy pointed to him and called him forward. As he walked toward Cindy, Jon felt sure he was in trouble—as though God was going to publicly rebuke him. But as Cindy began to deliver the prophecy, he could barely believe the words! She told of how the Lord had given Jon the heart of a pastor and how He was going to use Jon in days ahead to see mighty things happen for the kingdom of God!

Jon was stunned. There was no word of rebuke. His secret life was not uncovered. Cindy had prophesied to him about his destiny rather than his addictions. The words were so powerful that Jon was completely delivered that very night from alcoholism and addiction to tobacco. Today Jon is a governing elder in his church, a cell group leader, and is actively involved in implementing city-taking strategies where he lives. Jon will tell you that the turning point in his life was the night when God showed him his redemptive purpose rather than condemning him for his shortcomings. That is redemptive prophecy in action!

**5. Direction.** As we see throughout the Bible, prophets are given to bring direction to God's people. I have known my co-author, Rebecca Sytsema, for many years. In the early '90s we both served on Cindy Jacobs' staff at Generals of Intercession. During that time, Rebecca went through a two-year period of intensive healing in her life over many issues. I knew that the healing process had brought her to a place where she was ready for marriage. In early 1994, we were preparing to go to a conference in California. One day I looked at her and said, "You need to be at that conference. God has your husband waiting there!"

My words confirmed a feeling that she had been having for about a week, but she had not made her hotel reservations. I immediately picked up the phone and called the hotel where the rest of us were staying. I was told there were no rooms left. I simply told the woman on the phone that first of all Rebecca's father, Peter Wagner, was in charge of the conference, and secondly, her husband would be waiting for her there. The woman on the phone checked again and found one room left. It was at that conference that Rebecca met Jack Sytsema, God's perfect match for her. Two years later I had the privilege of performing their wedding.

This is a case in which God gave a clear word of direction and then made a way to see His prophesied will come to pass.

## THE PROCESS OF PROPHECY

Besides the functions of prophecy, it is important to understand the process of prophecy—that is, how it works in our lives on an ongoing basis. Here are three important elements of the process of prophecy in our lives:

**1. Prophecy is incomplete.** "For we know in part and we prophesy in part" (1 Cor. 13:9). No personal or corporate word of prophecy is complete in and of itself. In his excellent book, *Developing Your Prophetic Gifting*, Graham Cooke says, "God only reveals what we need to know in order to do his will in that particular time and place. The things that he does not wish us to know, he keeps secret from the one prophesying. Elisha said, 'The Lord has hidden it from me!' (2 Kings 4:27). In other words, 'I don't know.'"[1]

God may give us a little bit here and a little bit there. In retrospect, we may wonder why God didn't tell us this or that, or why He did tell us some seemingly unimportant detail. God always knows what He is doing when He reveals His heart to us through prophecy. That is something that we must simply trust. We must bear in mind, however, that we do not know all we may encounter, or how the prophecies may be fulfilled. Prophecy may point out a path, but we must follow the Lord daily and trust in Him as we move ahead along that path.

**2. Prophecy evolves.** As we follow the Lord in obedience, He will give us our next piece. He will not tell us what He wants us to do three steps down the road. He gives it to us step-by-step. Such was the case with Abraham. God gave him a piece here and a piece there. Each time Abraham obeyed, God would speak to him again until He brought him into the fullness of what He wanted to do. God would confirm, expand, give new insights and move Abraham on to his next place.

That is the way of prophecy. Each prophetic word is incomplete, yet as we are faithful to obey God, we receive new pieces of the puzzle. Prophecies will build on earlier prophecies to bring confirmation and fresh understanding.

**3. Prophecy is provisional.** The key to the process of prophecy is obedience. God will not usurp our wills and force us to follow His will. Mary, for instance, could have said no to the prophetic pronouncement that she would become pregnant. Instead, she responded by saying, "Behold the maidservant of the Lord! Let it be to me according to your word" (Luke 1:38). Had she said no, the Holy Spirit would never have forced her to become pregnant! Although she did not completely understand how this would happen, nor did she probably not grasp the magnitude of what she had been chosen for, nevertheless, she knew that through the prophetic word God had revealed His destiny for her life. Through her choice of obedience, the word came to pass and the human race has been blessed ever since.

## THE VALUE OF PROPHECY

Prophecy is a tremendous gift that God has given to His Church. It is full of important benefits for us, both individually and corporately. Here is a list of some of the values of receiving this gift into our lives and churches:

**1. Prophecy brings healing.** Proverbs 25:11 says, "A word fitly spoken is like apples of gold in settings of silver." Accepting the comfort and edification available through prophecy can heal a broken heart. As Graham Cooke writes, "Hurts, wounds, rejections and emotional trauma are a part of our lives, both before and after salvation. The Good News is that we serve a God who is committed to our healing at every level (physical, mental, emotional). The goal of God is wholeness of life and fullness of the Spirit. Prophecy is a wonderful part of that healing and renewing process. Prophecy brings us, by direct verbal communication, into contact with God's real perspective on our lives and current situations."[2]

**2. Prophecy deepens our relationship with God.** When we ponder how the God of all creation cares enough to send a personal message from His heart, no matter what the function of the prophecy, it causes us to stop and think about what our individual value to Him must be! Receiving His word brings a new appreciation of God's deep love and care for us. It reminds us of our position with Him. As in any relationship, communication is a key to reaching deeper levels. When God communicates with us, and we respond to Him, our relationship becomes deeper and more meaningful.

**3. Prophecy provides direction and renewed vision.** When we receive God's word, we often get a clearer understanding of where He is leading us. Knowing where we are headed causes us to focus more intently on the plans and goals God has for us. New excitement and vision are often direct results of the prophetic word that brings us direction.

**4. Prophecy brings biblical insight.** As we will see in the next chapter, prophecy must line up with the written Word of God. That being the case, the revelation that comes through prophecy will often open up new insights and inspire deeper understanding of mysteries in the Bible. Paul says that we can gain "knowledge in the mystery of Christ which in other ages was not made known to the sons of men, as it has now been revealed by the Spirit to His holy apostles and prophets" (Eph. 3:4-5). Prophecy will often serve as a catalyst for understanding biblical truths that we have not seen or understood before.

**5. Prophecy confirms.** God has a number of ways He uses to communicate with us. It may come through reading Scripture or hearing a message or counseling with a friend.  God delights in confirming His message to us.  He will often use prophecy to say something to us that we may have heard in some other form.

**6.  Prophecy can warn.**  God does not want us ensnared by our own sin or by schemes of the devil.  Prophecy, delivered in love, can often warn us that our own sin will result in calamity and despair down the road if we do not repent and turn to God. Prophecy can also warn us of traps the enemy has set for us. After the birth of Jesus, the wise men were warned not to return to Herod (Matt. 2:12).  Then Mary and Joseph were prophetically warned to flee to Egypt and stay there until the Lord spoke to them again in order to spare Jesus from Herod's plot to kill Him (Matt. 2:13).  Paul was warned by Jesus in Acts 22:18, "Make haste and get out of Jerusalem quickly, for they will not receive your testimony concerning Me."  Because God sees the destiny He has for us, He often uses the prophetic word to warn us of the snares the enemy has set up to destroy our destined purposes.

**7.  Prophecy can bring salvation.**  As I mentioned in Chapter One, when I was 11 years old, I heard the voice of the Lord say, "This is your day."  That was the day of my salvation.  All salvation is a result of hearing the voice of the Lord on some level.  Yet there are times when the Lord clearly speaks.  Graham Cooke writes, "I have seen many atheists and agnostics persuaded by God through prophecy.  It is the work of the Spirit to convict of sin (John 16:8-11).  Prophecy can uncover past history which needs to be amended.  It can provide an agenda for repentance, restitution, and revival."[3]

**8. Prophecy releases new practices into the Church.**  There is nothing new under the sun, but there are diverse administrations.  The administration of the 13th century will not work in the 21st century.  By "new practices," I do not mean a departure from the Apostles' Creed.  But there are new methods of operation and administration that God is revealing to the Church that will burst us forth into new practices and new strategies that will work for the 21st century.

**9. Prophecy provides insight into counseling.** When I am involved in a counseling situation, I rely on the prophetic voice of God to provide me with the understanding I need to give godly wisdom. The Lord will often reveal to me what the problem is, what the root is, and give me a prophetic word to unlock the strategy that the person needs to move forward in God's plan for their life. It has proven to be a very effective method of counseling.

**10. Prophecy shows us how to pray.** When we know the will of God in a certain area, we have great fuel for our prayer lives. God's will is made known to us through the prophetic. That knowledge gives us a basis for ongoing prayer to see His will done on earth as it is in heaven.

**11. Prophecy releases strategy for warfare.** Praying through a prophetic word can often involve spiritual warfare. Timothy 1:18 says, "This charge I commit to you, son Timothy, according to the prophecies previously made concerning you, that by them you may wage the good warfare." Joshua also received prophetic instruction on the warfare he was to wage in order to see the walls of Jericho fall (Josh. 6:1-5). Prophecy can provide us with the strategy we need to war against the enemy who strives to keep God's plans from manifesting in our lives.

**12. Prophecy stirs faith.** Prophecy can change things. When our spirits receive a word from the Lord, we know that there is hope, that there is a way to see that prophetic word fulfilled. Remember how Jon was freed from alcoholism when Cindy gave him a redemptive prophecy? Jon's faith for seeing God deliver him and bring him into his destiny skyrocketed that day! That is the power of prophecy. In Chapter Five we will discuss the relationship between prophecy and faith in greater detail.

---

[1] Graham Cooke, *Developing Your Prophetic Gifting* (Kent, England: Sovereign World, Ltd., 1994) p. 119.

[2] Ibid., pp. 30-31.

[3] Ibid. pp. 39-40.

CHAPTER FOUR

# TESTING THE PROPHETIC WORD

There are many ways you can receive a prophetic word from the Lord. You may have an impression in your spirit, or the Lord may illuminate a passage of Scripture that has particular significance in your life, or you may have a vivid, prophetic dream. Prophecy can also come when someone is communicating wisdom and counsel that gives you the direction you are looking for in your life. Someone may even say, "I believe the Spirit of God is saying this to you." Prophecy can also come by God or angelic beings visiting you and giving supernatural revelation. These are all sound, biblical methods which God uses at different times to speak to His children.

## PROPHECY HAS BOUNDARIES

There are several things we must be aware of as we begin to move into receiving prophetic words. We must understand that prophecy has boundaries that God has established for our own protection. For instance, in a corporate setting, Paul gives the following guideline: "Let two or three prophets speak, and let the others judge" (1 Cor. 14:29).

Another boundary is set in 1 Thessalonians 5:19-21, "Do not

quench the Spirit. Do not despise prophecies. Test all things; hold fast what is good." The rest of this chapter is devoted to applying tests to prophetic words so that we can hold fast to what is good.

## IS MY WORD FROM GOD?

Not every voice we hear is from the Holy Spirit. Satan has the ability to counterfeit gifts in order to bring confusion and get us off course. His ability to counterfeit includes the gift of prophecy. Jeremiah records the Lord saying, "I have not sent these prophets, yet they ran. I have not spoken to them, yet they prophesied" (Jer. 23:21).

That still happens. There are false prophets. That is why we are admonished to test all things and hold onto what is good. Here are some unclean sources of prophetic words that we need to be aware of:

**1. The occult.** "You are wearied in the multitude of your counsels; let now the astrologers, the stargazers, and the monthly prognosticators stand up and save you from what shall come upon you" (Isa. 47:13). Occultic sources of prophecy include psychics, tarot cards, Ouija boards, astrology and horoscopes, clairvoyants, mediums, ESP, witchcraft, divination, and so forth. These sources of prophetic utterance must be avoided completely!

**2. Delusions.** "How long will this be in the heart of the prophets who prophesy lies? Indeed they are prophets of the deceit of their own heart" (Jer 23:26). Not everyone that gives you a false prophecy is malicious, they are just confused. Sometimes they are walking in their own delusion, thinking they are hearing God when they are not.

**3. Unrestrained desires.** Desires are a natural function of the human emotion. Desires are linked with our wishes, aspirations, urges, and expectations. Gone unchecked, desires can cause us to rebel against the will of God in our lives. Have you ever heard anyone use the expression, "yearning desire"? Many times we can so yearn to have something that we will listen for any voice that will align with our desires. False prophecy can, therefore, come through a desire so unrestrained that we can no longer discern the voice of the Lord over the voice of the enemy or our own flesh. Prophecy can come out of the longings of someone's heart, rather than from a pure word from the Lord.

**4. Manipulation and control.** "Likewise, son of man, set your face against the daughters of your people, who prophesy out of their own heart; prophesy against them" (Ezek. 13:17). Prophecy has been used to try and manipulate people into actions they may not otherwise take. For instance, someone might want this person to marry that person. It seems like a good thing— so good, in fact, that God must want it too, so they may go up to one or the other and say, "The Lord says you are to marry _____." The true origin behind the word was not God, but a manipulative and controlling spirit. We will discuss this more later on.

**5. Immaturity.** There are true prophets that have not yet matured in their gifting that may deliver a word from the Lord mixed with their own emotions. Therefore, the word is impure. This is where some sifting needs to take place, and we are to "hold fast to what is good."

**6. False dreams.** "Behold, I am against those who prophesy false dreams" (Jer. 23:32). The enemy is able to counterfeit prophetic dreams, just as he is able to counterfeit prophetic words. We must realize that when we are asleep, we are not fully active in our spirit. Many times the enemy will use this time to speak false words to us.

**7. Demons.** "And I have seen folly in the prophets of Samaria: they prophesied by Baal and caused My people Israel to err" (Jer. 23:13). Just as the Lord can send angels to prophesy, the enemy can also send one of his hosts (Baal was sent in the biblical example given) to deliver a demonic prophecy.

## JUDGING PROPHECY

There are many origins for what may seem like prophecy from God. So how do you know if what is being said is from God? How do we test prophecy? Here is a list that has been compiled partly from Graham Cooke's *Developing Your Prophetic Gifting*, along with my own experience in judging prophecy:

**1. Does the word you have received edify, exhort, and comfort you?** Does it accomplish the basic functions we outlined in the last chapter? 1 Corinthians 14:3 says that the real purpose of prophecy is to edify, exhort, and comfort. If the word leaves you with a sense of uneasiness instead of edification, or you feel that something is just not right, you should not receive the word without further testing.

**2. What is the spirit behind the prophecy?** Someone might begin to speak a word to you, but the spirit behind the word does not seem right. It may have a spirit of condemnation on it. Even though it could be totally true, if you feel weighed down and condemned you may need to judge it further. Remember, the spirit in which all prophecy should be given is love. Therefore, even a word of exhortation or correction should leave you with a freedom to rebuild.

**3. Does it conform to Scripture?** God is not going to say one thing in the Bible and then tell you the opposite in a prophetic word. The prophetic word of the Lord will *always* line up with the inspired, written Word of God that has been given to us as a guide and an example. Remember, the Bible has no bounds or time frame. Therefore, you will find that the principles and the illumination of the Word of God are just as important for us today as when it was written. In other words, your example or Scriptural principle may be found in the Old Testament as often as in the New Testament. But if someone gives you a word and you find no Scriptural principle, basis, or example for that word in the Bible, please do not fully embrace the word.

**4. Does it display the character of Christ?** In her book, *The Voice of God*, Cindy Jacobs says, "Sometimes wolves in sheep's clothing manipulate Scripture for their own purposes. Just because someone is quoting chapter and verse to you doesn't make a prophecy accurate. Even if Scripture is being used, another area to check is to make sure Christ's character shines through the prophetic word."[1] This, again, leads to love. In addition to love, prophetic words should also exalt Jesus rather than a person or ministry. They should lead us to His feet rather than to an organization.

**5. Is it manipulative or controlling?** Even though some words are filled with truth, they can manipulate or control a person under the desire of the one giving the word. Control and manipulation are used to wield power, abuse, dominate, or rule over others. Such a word has no love, much less any of the other fruit of the spirit, and should be discarded.

**6. Does it usurp your will?** Does the word say you *must* do this or that? If so, there should be a red flag. God gives us all freedom—even the freedom to sin. All prophetic words should leave you the choice to either accept them or reject them.

**7. Does it pull rank?** In other words, does the word begin to move you out of the authoritative structure in which God has placed you? Does it breed rebellion against authority, produce suspicion or insubordination? God gave each of His children an authority structure in which to operate. If the word suggests that you supercede biblical authority, reject it!

**8. Does it confirm what God is saying to you?** God is always willing to confirm His word to us. When God gives a word, He will usually give it over and over again in many forms. Prophetic words often confirm what God has already spoken to you, and fit in with what He is doing in your life.

**9. Does it allow outside perspective?** If someone gives you a word and says that you are not supposed to communicate it with anyone else, be careful. That is a violation of Scripture. Remember that 1 Thessalonians tells us that any word of God is to be evaluated. Godly counsel is always in order, particularly when the word tells you something drastic, like quit your job and move to another city. Proverbs tells us there is wisdom in a multitude of counselors, and that includes judging the prophetic. In fact, a good test of any prophecy is to take it to a mature spiritual friend or authority in your life and ask them to help you judge the word.

**10. Does it give a dire warning?** Warnings are fine, but see what kind of a warning it is. Is the warning so dire that you have no way out and it produces hopelessness in you, or does the warning show you your way of escape? Is there redemption?

Cindy Jacobs tells the story of one such warning that I prophesied over Houston, Texas, on September 21, 1994. The word was, " *'I would say, the next 24 days are critical.* Though the enemy has stood against you as a city, I have brought you to a crossroads and you are about to make a transition and crossover. My eyes are upon this city and the remnant of this city, and I will overcome the structures that are set against My Spirit in this city. Revelation that has been withheld is going to begin to come down to people like rain. *Look to the river of the east.* As that river rises so will My people.

" '…Watchman, what do you see? He replied, *'I see a fire. It is a literal fire. Fire is on the river'* Then the Lord said, 'My fire will begin to come to this city.'

" 'I would call you to the night watch. Gather together in the night watch. Sing in the night in the hard areas of the city and evil will be uncovered and deliverance will come. If you will enter into the night watch, you will overthrow the impending destruction and doom that is set for the area.'

"One of the prayer leaders, Deborah DeGar, took the prophetic word from church to church, leading a prayer watch from 3:00-6:00 a.m. *At the end of 24 days, it began to rain in Houston.* There had never been a flood exactly like it in the history of the city. Houston was brought before the eyes of the nation. The San Jacinto River *(the river to the east)* began to rise and flood the entire territory. Gas lines erupted underneath the river and the flooded river *literally had a fire that burned in its midst.* In the middle of the chaos, the Church came together in great unity.

"In the case of this prophetic warning, the flooding was not averted, but it did not do the damage it could have done."[2]

**11. How do you feel about the word in your spirit?** God has given each of us discernment in our spirits. If we receive a prophetic word, and it just doesn't seem right to us, for whatever reason, we have cause to check it out further before we embrace it as a word from the Lord.

**12. Is it confirmed by the church?** If a word is given in a corporate setting, there should be instant feedback from the people and the leaders. There should be a corporate "amen" that comes forth. Rebecca Sytsema, my co-author, was once in a meeting in the Anaheim Vineyard when a man stood up during worship to give a prophetic word. He said that the Lord was longing to fulfill the desire of His children's hearts. He said that God was, in fact, a God who longed to bring even what seems like fairy tales to pass. He finished his word and sat down. When worship concluded, John Wimber came to the microphone. After a moment of silence, he simply stated, "Our God is *not* a fairy tale God!" A loud round of applause went up from the crowd, many of whom had discerned that something had not been right with the word. If a word was given in a corporate setting, what was reaction of the leaders and of the congregation? If they seemed unwilling to embrace the word, you should consider doing the same.

**13. Does it come to pass?** "When a prophet speaks in the name of the LORD, if the thing does not happen or come to pass, that is the thing which the LORD has not spoken; the prophet has spoken it presumptuously" (Deut. 18:22). Here is, of course, one of the most basic tests of a prophetic word. Remember, prophecy may be conditional, based on something we must do. If you read through the list of responses in the next chapter, and are satisfied that you have done all that God has required of you concerning the word, and it is still not fulfilled, it may not have been a word from the Lord at all.

**14. Does it produce fruit?** A true word from the Lord will bear good fruit that we will be able to discern. In his book, *Proph-*

*ecy*, Bruce Yocum writes, "If we pay attention to the effect that prophetic utterances have, we can judge their worth. A word from the Lord will produce life, peace, hope, love, and all the other fruit of the Holy Spirit. A word which is not from the Lord will either produce the fruit of evil—strife, anger, jealousy, lust, indifference—or it will have no effect at all."[3] What kind of fruit has the prophetic word given to you produced in your life? This will be a telling factor in whether or not you accept it as a word from the Lord.

---

[1] Cindy Jacobs, *The Voice of God* (Ventura, CA: Regal Books, 1995), p. 76.

[2] Ibid., p. 181.

[3] Bruce Yocum, *Prophecy*, (Ann Arbor, MI: Word of Life, 1976), p. 119.

CHAPTER FIVE

# RESPONDING TO PROPHECY

Once we have tested a prophetic word and have come to the conclusion that God has spoken into our lives, we must then understand how to respond to what we have been told. Here is a helpful checklist of proper actions to take:

**1. Keep a journal.** There is tremendous importance in writing down, tape recording, or keeping some kind of record of prophetic words. Don't rely purely on your memory. Having a record of prophecy helps us to remember the whole word, keeps us from adding thoughts to the word, and builds our faith when we go back and read the word. We can also see how the word we receive fits in with what God has said to us in the past.

There are times, however, when we do not clearly understand all that God is trying to say to us at the time the word is given. Having a record of the word helps us go back and gain fresh understanding at a later time. For example, in June of 1998, I was given a birthday party at the home of C. Peter Wagner. Cindy Jacobs had come to help celebrate. During the party, Cindy began feeling a spirit of prophecy come upon her. Peter, who keeps a full prophetic journal, grabbed a tape recorder. Cindy gave me a beautiful word for the new year I was entering into in my own life. Then she turned to Peter and began to prophesy that God was calling him to raise up a seminary that would gather leaders from around the world. She went on to give several specific details.

At the time such a thought had never entered Peter's mind. He had no frame of reference for such a concept. Nonetheless, Cindy's word was transcribed and entered on page 67 of the Wagner Prophetic Journal. A few months later Peter met with several apostles from various streams of Christianity. During that meeting, the Lord spoke to Peter about a whole new concept for training leaders from around the world. It became clear that he was to retire from his position as a professor at Fuller Theological Seminary, where he had taught for 30 years, and begin his own seminary-type school. As he obeyed the Lord, God began pouring new revelation out as to how the school would operate. Later that year, he officially formed Wagner Leadership Institute, and the first student was enrolled that December.

Peter was able to go back to page 67 of his journal and revisit exactly what the Lord had spoken to him. In fact, as he began to seek counsel and set up the leadership for the school, he was able to distribute copies of Cindy's prophecy to him so that those involved would also know the word God had given over the new venture.

**2. Do not interpret the word by the desires of your flesh.** Many of God's people have fallen into deception by taking a prophetic word and adding their own interpretation to it, then saying that God promised them this or that. Cindy Jacobs offers the following caution: "I have had many singles come to me saying God has promised them certain mates because they were told so in prophecies. When I asked them what the prophecies said, they came up with something like, 'God said He would give me the desires of my heart and so-and-so is the desire of my heart.' (Such an interpretation) may be the desire of their flesh but God may not have anything to do with it at all."[1] Be very careful not to take a word and run in a direction God has not ordained.

**3. Embrace the word.** To embrace means to grab hold of something. When we embrace or grab hold of a word, it activates faith to see the word fulfilled. Remember that faith comes by hearing and hearing by the word of God (Rom. 10:17). When we embrace a true prophetic word, it brings faith that God has a destiny for us. We must allow ourselves to embrace our prophetic word with the faith that God is well able to do what He said He would do. If God has inspired the word, He will uphold it by the Holy Spirit. Even if we have received a difficult word, if the word is from God, faith will rise within our spirit because we know that God has a path for us.

When I was 18, the Lord spoke to me and said, "I have called you for the healing of the nations." At that time the only frame of reference I had for a call to the nations was to become a missionary, which was something I did not want to do. Even though I was willing to obey God, I did not embrace His word to me. It was 10 years later when God spoke that word to me again. This time I embraced the word fully. He then began to show me that He had not called me to be a missionary, but rather an intercessor, prophet, and strategist for the nations He would lay on my heart. He began to open doors for me to travel in and out of nations so that I could bring prophetic words and build up strategic intercession to see His will accomplished. Had I not been willing to embrace this word when He spoke it to me for a second time, I would have missed that portion of His destiny for my life.

**4. Pray it through.** Because prophecy is provisional, once we know what God wants to do in our lives, the best thing to do is to begin to pray along those lines. This will not only help to build our relationship to God and build persistence in faith, it can also teach us spiritual warfare. The enemy does not want to see God's will accomplished in our lives and will do all he can to see that we are not successful in reaching our destinies. That is why we must commit ourselves to praying through the word until we see it come to pass. For instance, I have known many barren couples who have received words about children. Yet they did not conceive immediately. In some cases, it took years. But as they chose to pray through their word with the faith that God is well able to do all that He says, the bondage of barrenness broke off not only their physical bodies, but often their spiritual lives as well.

**5. Obey the word.** As we mentioned in Chapter Three, prophecy is often provisional. That means that there is something we must do to see it come to pass. There are conditions to meet. Here is a good biblical example: *"If* My people who are called by My name will humble themselves, and pray and seek My face, and turn from their wicked ways, *then* I will hear from heaven, and will forgive their sin and heal their land" (2 Chron. 7:14, italics added). Does God want to forgive the sin and heal the land of His people? Of course! But they have something they must do in order to see that prophecy occur, namely, humble themselves, pray, seek His face, and turn from their wicked ways. Something that has been prophesied to us may never come to pass if we are not faithful to meet the conditions.

Earlier I told the story of how Rebecca was to go to the conference in order to meet Jack. Had she not gone to that conference, she could have missed meeting God's chosen mate. God surely could have arranged another way for them to meet, but there was a timing issue involved as well. Her obedience to the prophetic word kept her moving forward in God's timing and destiny for her life.

**6. Look for the fulfillment of the word.** Having completed steps one through five, we should look for and expect that the word will be fulfilled. John 1:14 speaks of the word becoming flesh. That is a good statement for the fulfillment of a prophetic word. God desires that His word be made flesh—that the intangible substance of a prophetic promise become a tangible reality in our lives. Many do not see their promise manifested because they do not know how to "watch" for the fulfillment of their word.

## CAN I PROPHESY?

While it is not within the scope of this booklet to give this question a thorough answer, the discussion of prophecy would not be complete without a brief look at who can prophesy. While not all of us are called as God's spokesmen on the earth, the fact is that we all prophesy, whether it is through sharing an encouraging word, edifying a friend, giving godly advice, or knowingly giving a prophetic word. Romans 12:6 says we prophesy according to our measure of faith. What measure of faith are you operating in? I want to encourage you to ask God right now to increase your faith.

If you are a believer in the Lord Jesus Christ, the Holy Spirit is made resident within you. You can now ask the Spirit of God to begin to speak through you, knowing that He can. You can also give Him liberty to begin to manifest His particular giftings within you, whether they are prophecy, helps, hospitality, teaching, or any of the gifts listed in Romans 12, 1 Corinthians 12, and Ephesians 4. All the gifts are greatly needed in the body of Christ—including yours!

## A FINAL WORD

We hope this small booklet will help you as you embrace the voice of God, and evaluate any word that comes to you. For further study on this topic we have included a recommended reading list on the following page. May our Lord richly bless you as you seek to hear His voice and obey His will for your life!

---

[1] Cindy Jacobs, *The Voice of God*, (Ventura, CA: Regal Books, 1995), pp. 83-84.

# RECOMMENDED READING

Bickle, Mike. *Growing in the Prophetic*. Orlando, FL: Creation House, 1996.

Cooke, Graham. *Developing Your Prophetic Gifting*. Kent, England: Sovereign World, 1994.

Deere, Jack. *Surprised by the Voice of God*. Grand Rapids, MI: Zondervan Publishing House, 1996.

Hamon, Bill. *Prophets and Personal Prophecy*. Shippensburg, PA: Destiny Image, 1987.

Jacobs, Cindy. *The Voice of God*. Ventura, CA: Regal Books, 1995.

Joyner, Rick. *The Prophetic Ministry*. Charlotte, NC: Morningstar Publications, 1997.

Lord, Peter. *Hearing God*. Grand Rapids, MI: Baker Books, 1988.

Payne, Leanne. *Listening Prayer*. Grand Rapids, MI: Baker Books, 1994.

Yocum, Bruce. *Prophecy*. Ann Arbor, MI: Servant Publications, 1976.

**Recommended Tape Series:**

*School of the Prophets*. Eight-tape set and manual featuring Chuck Pierce, Robert Heidler, Barbara Wentroble and Jim Hodges. Available through Glory of Zion Ministries, P.O. Box 1601, Denton, TX, 76201; phone 940-382-1166.

# INDEX

# What is
# Global Harvest Ministries?

There are still two billion individuals who are not within reach of the gospel and who do not yet have a vital, indigenous church movement. Global Harvest Ministries, under the leadership of Dr. C. Peter Wagner, unites existing national and international prayer networks in order to focus maximum prayer power on world evangelization; especially for the lost people of the 10/40 Window.

Working with Christian leaders all over the earth, Global Harvest is **seeking to bring together a massive prayer force** that is equipped, trained and focused for the fierce spiritual battles that will free millions of people from the grip of the enemy, and allow them to hear and receive the Gospel.

We are seeking those who will join hands with us in the following ways:

- **In Prayer:** Mobilizing intercession and prayer for the world's most spiritually impoverished peoples.

- **With Financial Help:** Monthly support is needed to mobilize this massive, worldwide prayer effort.

If you are interested in helping in these ways, or would like more information on Global Harvest Ministries please contact us at:

Global Harvest Ministries
P.O. Box 63060
Colorado Springs, CO 80962-3060
Phone: 719-262-9922
E-Mail: Info@globalharvest.org
Web Site: www.globalharvest.org

I  N  S  T  I  T  U  T  E
P  U  B  L  I  C  A  T  I  O  N  S

## RIDDING YOUR HOME
## OF SPIRITUAL DARKNESS
### Chuck D. Pierce
### & Rebecca Wagner Sytsema

Christians are often completely unaware of how the enemy has gained access to their homes through what they own. This practical, easy-to-read book can be used by any Christian to pray through their home and property in order to close the door to the enemy and experience richer spiritual life. Included are chapters on children, sin, generational curses, and spiritual discernment, as well as a step-by-step guide to praying through your home and a section of questions and answers.
Paperback (75 pp.) • 0.9667481.7.4 • **$7.20 (save 10%)**

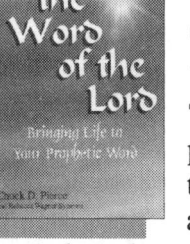

## RECEIVING THE WORD
## OF THE LORD
### Chuck D. Pierce
### & Rebecca Wagner Sytsema

The Bible makes it very clear that God has a plan for our lives. By hearing and receiving the voice of God, we can know our purpose and destiny. In this book you will discover how to hear the voice of God, develop an understanding of prophecy, learn how to test a prophetic word, and experience the joy of responding to God's voice.
Paperback (46 pp.) • 0.9667481.2.3 • **$5.40 (save 10%)**